Peas Publishing
P.O. Box 281
Oshtemo, MI 49077
peaspublishing@gmail.com

Illustrations Copyright © 2016 by Antara Majumder

Ordering Information:
Quantity sales. Special discounts are available on quantity purchases by corporations, associations, and others. For details, contact the publisher at the address above.

Orders by U.S. trade bookstores and wholesalers. Please contact Distribution: peaspublishing@gmail.com
Printed in the United States of America

Publisher's Cataloging-in-Publication data
Dickason, Keshia.
Peas in a Pod Series: Arianna's First 5K / Keshia Dickason
p. 28.

ISBN-13: 978-0692644478
ISBN-10: 0692644474
BISAC: Sports & Recreation / Running & Jogging First Edition


First Edition

## Hello Girls,

Have you ever run in a 5K or any race before? Well get ready to go on an exciting journey that will teach you the proper things to do when preparing for your first 5K run with fun.

In this book you will be able to:

- Read about Arianna's running experience.
- Journal your runs.
- Talk about your experiences.
- Learn helpful tips for healthy living.
- Read inspirational quotes.
- Have fun.

## Girl Power Tip

Grab a comfortable reading space and get ready to read and journal while gaining more Girl Power.

This is the story about a young girl named Arianna who wanted to run in her first 5K run. The 5K run is a long-distance road running competition over a distance of five kilometers (3.1 miles). Also referred to as the 5K road race, 5 km, or simply 5K, it is the shortest of the most common road running distances. It is usually distinguished from the 5000 meters track running event by stating the distance in kilometers, rather than meters.

Arianna is an elementary student that wanted to run in the Girls On The Run annual 5K. This run is for girls in 3rd through 6th grade. She became interested in the Girls On the Run 5K when she first attended a Girls On The Run event with her mom and loved the excitement and joy she found in watching each girl cross the finish line. Seeing the smiles and cheers that the crowd gave each girl after they finished the run was amazing.

She said to her mom that she wanted to run in the next Girls On The Run annual 5K. Her mom agreed that it would be a great idea for her and her friends to run. Arianna was so excited and could not wait to run her first 5K run! When she returned to school she encouraged all her friends to sign up to participate in the Girls On the Run 5K. Her friends were excited and could not wait to start training for the run. The girls signed up for the program and were happy to start their new adventure together.

**Girl Power Tip**
Girls, remember when trying something new and exciting. Remember that it is ok to ask friends to join you, but it is also ok to do new and fun things alone.

When Arianna got home from school she went to her mom and asked for help to prepare for her first 5K. She told Arianna that she would need to train to get ready for her run, eat properly and would need proper running clothes. She told her it would be easy and fun to do. After hearing this Arianna was so happy and ready to run. Her mom told her that she needed a few things before she could start her training for her very "big, special" 5K run.

1. **Running Shoes and Socks.** Proper running shoes are important to protect and support your feet and ankles during runs. You always want to have shoes that have a good grip and strong sole. Slippery shoes can cause you to fall or hurt yourself. Socks that support your entire foot during running is important for protection.

2. **Comfortable running clothes.** Comfortable clothes that are not too tight are best for running because they allow your body to move freely. Never wear jeans or tight clothing when exercising. Comfortable running and exercise clothing can be T-shirt or sweat shirt, shorts or jogging pants.

3. **Hats or Headbands** to keep sun or hair out of your face. Sometimes Sunscreen may be applied to the body when needed to avoid sun burn.

**Girl Power Tip**
Remember to always be comfortable and never wear anything that will be heavy or distract you while running. Do not wear items that could block your eyes or things that could fall off of your body and make you trip or fall during your run. Your safety is important.

Training begins on the track and in the gym when it rains. Before the girls practice, it is important for them to have a "nice, healthy snack." The girls will train for this run for 8 weeks.

The girls have circle time with their coach before they start to stretch and exercise. "In circle time, the girls share positive words of encouragement to give them motivation and help build their leadership skills." The coach informs the girls that they are all super stars and they can do anything they want to do and be anything they want to be!

**Girl Power Tip**

Today is your day
To Start Fresh
To Eat Right
To Train Hard
To Live Healthy
To Be Proud

by Bonnie Pfisher

Arianna talked to her mom, who is also a Girls on the Run coach, about her day at practice and how fun it is to get ready for the 5K run. She told her mom that she loved to be with other girls, doing positive things that gave her "GIRL POWER" every time she attends practice. Her mom was happy to hear all the positive things that were going on at practice. She reminds Arianna that she can also be a leader outside of practice and use what she learns in practice in her everyday life to help motivate others. Arianna smiled and told her mom that she would be kind to everyone and tell all girls that they can be Rock Stars and help everyone they meet.

**Girl Power Tip**

Always encourage others to do good. Be positive role models to anyone you meet and use your "Girl Power" to do good! You are all leaders.

10

Arianna becomes tired while running her laps during practice and then she remembers her mom's words. She remembers that each day she may become tired but that her mom and coaches have always told her that it is OK to slow down - but to keep moving.

**Girl Power Tip**

Remember to do your laps for you. You don't have to compete with anyone - run at your own pace. It doesn't matter how fast you go, just as long as you keep moving. Girl Power is the best power to have!

# Write in your laps below.

Date: _____

Date: _____

Date: _____

Date: _____

Date: _____

Date: _____

Date: _____

Date: _____

Date: _____

Date: _____

Date: _____

Date: _____

Lap: _____

Lap: _____

Lap: _____

Lap: _____

Lap: _____

Lap: _____

Lap: _____

Lap: _____

Lap: _____

Lap: _____

Lap: _____

Lap: _____

# Write in your laps below.

Date: _____     Lap: _____

Date: _____     Lap: _____

Date: _____     Lap: _____

Date: _____     Lap: _____

Date: _____     Lap: _____

Date: _____     Lap: _____

Date: _____     Lap: _____

Date: _____     Lap: _____

Date: _____     Lap: _____

Date: _____     Lap: _____

Date: _____     Lap: _____

Date: _____     Lap: _____

# Write in your laps below.

Date: _____     Lap: _____

Date: _____     Lap: _____

Date: _____     Lap: _____

Date: _____     Lap: _____

Date: _____     Lap: _____

Date: _____     Lap: _____

Date: _____     Lap: _____

Date: _____     Lap: _____

Date: _____     Lap: _____

Date: _____     Lap: _____

Date: _____     Lap: _____

Date: _____     Lap: _____

# Write in your laps below.

| Date: _____ | Lap: _____ |
| Date: _____ | Lap: _____ |
| Date: _____ | Lap: _____ |
| Date: _____ | Lap: _____ |
| Date: _____ | Lap: _____ |
| Date: _____ | Lap: _____ |
| Date: _____ | Lap: _____ |
| Date: _____ | Lap: _____ |
| Date: _____ | Lap: _____ |
| Date: _____ | Lap: _____ |
| Date: _____ | Lap: _____ |
| Date: _____ | Lap: _____ |

# Race Day

Arianna is at the end of the eight weeks of training and it is the day of the Big Girls on the Run 5K. The girls are transported to the meeting location for the run from their schools to get ready to run. All of the girls from all over the city are excited, smiling and ready to run. The coaches gather the girls together and give them a nice talk to help them in the run.

**Girl Power Tip**

Remember to be safe at all times.

Remember that if you are tired you can slow down and walk until you feel like running again. Remember to look for coaches on the running trail if you need help with anything.

Remember you are all winners, Girls Run the World, Go and Make your Mark!

**You did Your First 5K Run!**
**Collect your Medal!**

**The End**

# Write about the feelings you had after running your first 5K Run.

_____

_____

_____

_____

_____

_____

_____

_____

_____

_____

_____

_____

# Track all of your future runs here

| Name of Run | Date of Run | Time or Distance of Run |
|---|---|---|

1. _____
2. _____
3. _____
4. _____
5. _____
6. _____
7. _____
8. _____
9. _____
10. _____
11. _____
12. _____
13. _____
14. _____
15. _____
16. _____
17. _____
18. _____
19. _____
20. _____

# Inspirational Running Quotes

 When your legs are tired Run with your heart

 Girls Run the World

 It doesn't matter who wins, It matters that you finish

Author: Keshia Dickason
Born: Springhill, LA
Raised in: Muskegon, MI

Running became a part of her family life shortly after her daughter, Arianna, finished her first 5K run in 2009. In 2014, she completed 40 5K Runs for her 40th birthday and the feeling of running in the wind touched her heart, soul and mind forever. Keshia says, "Running makes me feel in control, powerful and that I can conquer the world." Her youngest son loves track and her husband ran in college. "Our home is based on hard work and dedication. We work hard and play harder." As a new author, she prays that all youth and parents that read Arianna's First 5K will be inspired and motivated to incorporate a healthy lifestyle and daily exercise to help their families to remain healthy and fit together - mentally, emotionally and physically .

*"Run Your Race at Your Own Pace"*
*~ Keshia Dickason*

# NOTES

# NOTES

# NOTES

# NOTES

Made in the USA
San Bernardino, CA
01 April 2017